THE TRUTH ABOUT MARIJUANA

FREDERICK C. GROSS and REEVE CHACE

ROSEN PUBLISHING
New York

Published in 2012 by The Rosen Publishing Group, Inc.
29 East 21st Street, New York, NY 10010

First Edition

Library of Congress Cataloging-in-Publication Data

Gross, Frederick C., 1944–
The truth about marijuana / Frederick C. Gross, Reeve Chace.—1st ed.
p. cm.—(Drugs & consequences)
Includes bibliographical references and index.
ISBN 978-1-4488-4639-9 (library binding)
1. Marijuana—Juvenile literature. 2. Marijuana abuse—Juvenile literature.
I. Chace, Reeve. II. Title.
HV5822.M3G756 2012
613.8'35—dc22

2010045972

Manufactured in the United States of America

CPSIA Compliance Information: Batch #S11YA: For further information, contact Rosen Publishing, New York, New York, at 1-800-237-9932.

CONTENTS

Marijuana is one of the most widely used drugs in the United States today. According to the National Survey on Drug Use and Health, in 2009, almost 21.8 million people who were age twelve or older in the United States were current users of illegal drugs. Of these 21.8 million, approximately 77 percent used marijuana, and of these users, it was the only drug used by 58 percent of them. Results of the 2009 Monitoring the Future survey showed that, of high school seniors, 20.6 percent had smoked marijuana in the past month, 32.8 percent had smoked it in the past year, and 42 percent had smoked it in their lifetime.

Regular use of marijuana can have serious consequences, including loss of short-term memory, distorted perception, loss of coordination, increased heart rate, and anxiety and panic attacks. As reported by *Science Daily*, the results of a study in 2010 showed that overuse of marijuana can cause serious negative effects on the development of the teenage mind. Teens who smoke marijuana have a much harder time performing even simple tasks, according to a joint study presented at the American Academy of Pediatrics in 2008. Teens who use marijuana regularly not

Medical researchers believe that the smoke from a marijuana joint holds several of the same cancer-causing chemicals as those contained in tobacco smoke from a cigarette.

only perform badly at activities that involve certain parts of the brain, but the damage may have long-lasting effects. Studies also show that marijuana is a dangerous, potentially habit-forming drug. Many myths surround this drug. Don't believe anyone who tells you that recreational use of marijuana is safe.

It is believed that marijuana smoke contains some of the same cancer-causing chemicals as those found in cigarette smoke. According to the National Institutes of Health, studies show that someone who smokes five marijuana cigarettes each week may be taking in as many cancer-causing chemicals as someone who smokes a full pack of cigarettes every day. Marijuana can cause problems in your respiratory, immune, and reproductive systems.

Marijuana can also affect regular users psychologically. Users may begin to lose interest in other aspects of their lives. They stop caring about school and their future. They stop hanging out with friends and often spend their days doing nothing. Perhaps the most dangerous effect of marijuana is that people who experiment with it sometimes go on to use hard drugs. A marijuana user may experiment with a variety of harder drugs and may even become addicted.

Marijuana can lead to dependency and mental illness in teens. Teens who have been depressed at some point in the past year are more than twice as likely to have used marijuana as teens who have not reported being depressed, claims a report by the White House Office of National Drug Control

Policy. The report also said that smoking pot increases the risk of mental illness by 40 percent. Moreover, teens who smoke pot at least once every month over a yearlong period are three times more likely to have suicidal thoughts than those who don't.

In addition, the average potency of marijuana has risen to 10 percent, its highest level in history. A high concentration of THC (the drug's psychoactive ingredient) can have far more serious effects, especially on frequent users, than lower concentrations. Long-term effects include strong feelings of unhappiness, paranoia, and irritability. Plus, the higher potency is leading to an increase in admissions to emergency rooms and drug treatment programs.

You may hear that marijuana is dangerous or that it is harmless; that it can hurt you or help you; that it is addictive or nonaddictive. Only by knowing the facts can you make informed choices about your health and safety.

CHAPTER 1 MARIJUANA AND ITS USES

The scientific name for the marijuana plant is *Cannabis sativa*. Marijuana is actually the Spanish word for it; the word for the plant in English is hemp. It has many slang names, among them grass, pot, weed, ganja, herb, reefer, trees, the chronic, bud, dope, mary jane, and smoke.

Marijuana is a tall, strong-smelling plant that can grow just about anywhere. Because of its strength and because it is so easy to find and grow, hemp has been used for centuries to make paper, rope, and clothing.

Marijuana Plants and Their Chemicals

The amounts of chemicals in marijuana plants vary greatly. They differ depending on where the plant grows, the time of year, and even the time of day. That's why plants grown in Mexico have so many more chemicals than those grown in the United States. That's also why there are different qualities of marijuana; depending on where the plant was grown, it will affect you to a greater or lesser degree.

Marijuana contains more than four hundred different chemicals. However, only one chemical is responsible for the feeling you get from using marijuana. This chemical is called tetrahydrocannabinol (THC). THC expands the blood vessels in the lungs and in the brain, letting more oxygen into the rest of the system. It lowers the blood pressure and speeds up the heart. Because of the lowered blood pressure, less blood flows into the brain. This is why you feel light-headed, or high. It's something like hyperventilating.

THC is also the reason that marijuana is classified as a psychotropic drug. This means that it has the power to change the way you experience the world around you; it distorts your perception of reality. It can make you feel good, or it can make you feel scared and paranoid. It is difficult to be sure that what

Parts of a marijuana plant are harvested in different ways, depending on what a particular part will be used for. People cultivate the herb for making industrial fiber, seed oil, medicines, and drugs.

you're seeing, hearing, or feeling is really there when you are high on marijuana.

The most common form of marijuana sold is a mixture of leaves, seeds, and stems. The seeds and stems are removed,

and the leaves are most often smoked in a marijuana cigarette, or "joint." The process of smoking marijuana is known as getting high, or toking. Being high on marijuana also has many different slang names, such as "stoned," "baked," and "fried." People who use marijuana are known as potheads, dope heads, druggies, burnouts, and stoners. The butts of joints, called roaches, contain the most THC of the joint. These can be smoked using a roach clip. Sometimes marijuana is smoked in other ways, too. It can be smoked in a pipe. It can be smoked in a bong, a jar or plastic tube with water in the bottom to filter the smoke. Usually pipes and bongs are used with stronger marijuana to avoid burning the lungs.

Sometimes the resin is pressed out of the plant's leaves and hardened. Resin is a translucent, solid or semisolid substance that comes from plants. The cake produced from resin is called hashish, or hash. Such cakes are much stronger than the leaves alone. Distilled resin is called hash oil. This is the strongest form of marijuana. Often hash oil is put into food or drinks. Hash brownies, brownies made with hash oil, are a favorite food of users.

Proposition 19

On November 2, 2010, voters in the state of California rejected a proposition that would have allowed anyone over the age of twenty-one to possess up to 1 ounce (28.4 grams) of marijuana. The state law, which would have been the first state law in the nation to legalize marijuana, would have also allowed the growing of marijuana plants on property measuring up to 25 square feet (2.3 square meters). However, that would have been only under state law, if it had passed. U.S. federal law considers the act of smoking marijuana a crime. According to the *Los Angeles Times*, President Barack Obama stated that he is against legalizing marijuana and that his attorney general would vigorously enforce the U.S. Controlled Substances Act against people and organizations that possess, manufacture, or distribute marijuana for recreational use, even if those activities had been allowed under state law. In September 2010, the governor of California, Arnold Schwarzenegger, had already signed a bill that downgraded possession of less than 1 ounce (28.4 g) of marijuana from a misdemeanor to an infraction.

Critics of Proposition 19 believed that if the ballot measure had become law in California, it would have resulted in numerous legal problems and created regulatory upheaval for the state's cities and counties. They also believed that pot smokers would have gotten behind the wheel and shown up to work while high. Supporters of legalizing marijuana said that regulating and taxing the sale of pot would have helped raise money for the cash-poor local governments and save tens of millions of dollars each year in the cost of imprisonment and supervision of marijuana offenders. According to the Associated Press, proponents also believed that legalizing marijuana would have eased the drug-related violence in Mexico by causing marijuana prices to fall, and that it would lower marijuana-related arrests that they said were unfairly targeting young minorities.

Trends in Marijuana Use

Marijuana was known for its mind-altering properties as far back as 2737 BCE. It was common in China and India. It was not used as a drug in America for many years. It was called ditch weed because it could be found in just about any ditch in the country. The plant was mostly used for making cloth. Then, during World War I (1914–1918), Mexican migrant workers began bringing it with them to the United States. Marijuana has been brought across the Mexican-American border ever since. Owning marijuana was made a crime in 1937, when Congress passed the Marijuana Tax Act. The drug was still somewhat common, however, despite the law.

In the 1960s, a time of civil protest, many American youths were trying to change what they thought to be stuffy, old-fashioned morality. Many people involved in these protests smoked marijuana and their actions changed many outdated laws and opened the minds of many. Even less was known about the drug then, and even more people believed the myth that marijuana was not harmful. Many youths also felt that smoking it made as much of a statement as marching in a protest. At the same time, Americans were suffering through the Vietnam War (1954–1975). Many soldiers in Vietnam began doing drugs because they were easy to get, and they needed an escape. Many of these soldiers brought their drug use home with them.

When marijuana became popular in the 1960s, it was much weaker than it is now. Since that time, marijuana use has been growing. American plants have been crossbred to create a new plant that has a THC level two to ten times higher than in foreign marijuana. Some of these types, nicknamed "skunk," contain 12 to 18 percent THC. Because the THC is a lot more concentrated, marijuana is much stronger than it was in the 1960s. Even worse, it is often combined with other drugs to get a different effect or to make it cheaper to produce. Today, if you buy marijuana from someone, you have no way of knowing what you are really getting. It is unlikely that it will be pure marijuana. It might have other drugs, such as PCP, also known as angel dust, mixed in that will cause different reactions and affect you even more than pot alone. You could even end up overdosing on PCP and not even know it was in your joint.

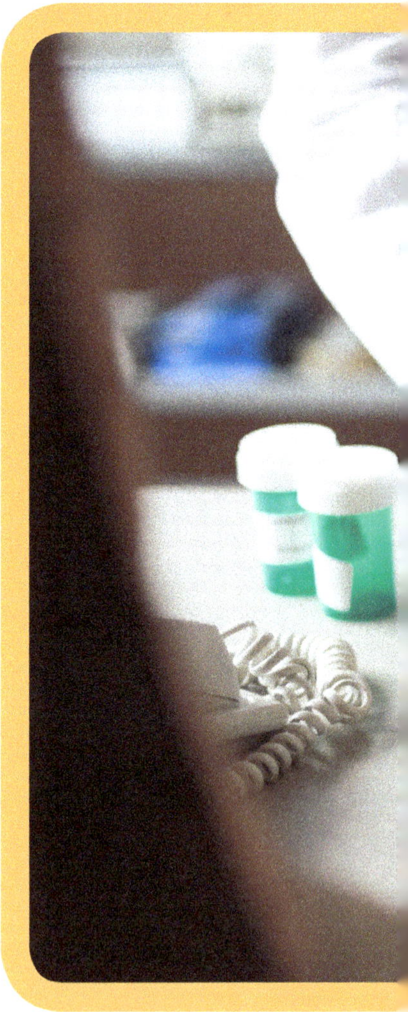

Sixty years ago, the federal government declared it illegal to use marijuana. Despite this, many people started using marijuana for medicinal purposes. Currently, twenty-six states and the District of Columbia have laws and resolutions that allow research on marijuana's medicinal use, allow doctors to prescribe marijuana to patients, or have asked the government to repeal the ban on the medical use of marijuana. These laws go directly against federal laws. Supporters

A pharmacist dispenses medical marijuana to a customer. In 2010, Arizona became the fifteenth U.S. state to legalize medical marijuana, even though the federal government has not approved medical marijuana's use.

of these laws believe that marijuana can help ease the pain of people suffering from illnesses such as acquired immunodeficiency syndrome (AIDS), cancer, and glaucoma. Those who oppose these laws say that there is no scientific evidence to prove the medicinal benefits of marijuana.

Marijuana is an easy drug for teens to get. Because of these current laws and marijuana's easy accessibility, marijuana is often the first drug that teens experiment with. Sixty percent of kids who smoke marijuana before the age of fifteen go on

DEA agents in Georgia arrested forty-five people and seized cash, guns, and nearly two tons of marijuana as part of an investigation into a Mexican drug trafficking cartel that used the Atlanta area as a distribution hub. The U.S. government aggressively fights the American marijuana trade, which has been valued at more than $113 billion per year.

to use cocaine. For this reason, marijuana is often called a "gateway" drug.

Most teenagers do not get marijuana from criminals or gang members. They get it from their friends. Often one person brings pot to a party and shares it with others. You may know someone who deals pot at your school. Marijuana is so common in the United States that it's easy to forget that it's illegal. However, you can be arrested for having just one joint.

Marijuana's Hidden Dangers

Governments in all countries are trying to stop the marijuana trade. They spray fields of marijuana with paraquat, a weed-killer. However, the drug growers don't want to lose their harvest, so they often sell the marijuana even after it's been sprayed with poison. Many people who have smoked weed laced with poison have become very sick, or even died.

Many people purposely buy marijuana that is laced with other drugs, such as PCP or cocaine. You can get laced marijuana without even knowing it. One kind of lace used is asthma medicine. For some people, this can cause extreme difficulty in breathing; those who smoke marijuana laced with asthma medicine have been known to faint, or even to fall into a coma. There is no way to tell normal marijuana from laced marijuana. It looks the same; it smells the same. It's only after you start getting sick that you realize what you smoked was laced.

A new form of laced marijuana has recently emerged: illy. This is marijuana laced with formaldehyde, a chemical used to preserve dead bodies. Obviously, it is not very good for live ones. Illy almost always makes the smoker very sick.

Most teenagers do not smoke marijuana every day. They might smoke at parties, or in social situations. The name for this type of user is a social user. Hardcore users, or stoners, however, use every day. They may have difficulty getting through a day without it. Most addicts don't pay attention to what's going on around them; the world is too confusing. They cannot keep their minds focused on one thing and instead mentally wander all over the place. They often have poor memories.

Smoking Hookah

Hookah, or water-pipe smoking, has become very popular among teens. Hookah is also known as narghile, shisha, and goza. It has a long history: hookah has been used for more than four hundred years across Asia and the Middle East.

You may think that smoking hookah is safer than smoking cigarettes or marijuana. But one half hour to an hour spent smoking hookah is equal to smoking a whole pack of cigarettes—in one sitting. According to the World Health Organization (WHO), one hour spent smoking hookah can expose you to high levels of toxic material including carbon monoxide, heavy metals, and cancer-causing chemicals. It can also expose you to nicotine.

Smoking hookah increases your blood pressure and heart rate. And some studies show that it can cause cancer in the lip, lungs, bladder, and stomach. If you add marijuana or hashish to the hookah—or use alcohol instead of water in the pipe—you're putting yourself at an even higher risk for health problems and for addiction.

Salvia divinorum is a hallucinogenic substance that can be rolled and smoked like a cigarette, chewed, or inhaled from a pipe or bong. The Drug Enforcement Administration claims that 1.8 million Americans who are twelve and older have used the herb in their lifetime.

Salvia Divinorum

Some parents and lawmakers are concerned that a hallucinogenic herb, called *Salvia divinorum*, may be the "next marijuana." *Salvia divinorum*, also called diviner's sage or just salvia, is native to Mexico—and is still grown there. It is most often smoked, but it can also be chewed or made into a tea and drunk. (*Salvia divinorum* is not the same as salvia, a common ornamental garden plant.)

Salvia divinorum impairs judgment and the ability to drive. Experts do not all agree on how its strength compares to that of marijuana. Although no known deaths have been attributed to its use, it has been listed as a factor in a Delaware teen's suicide. (Brett's Law is the statute in Delaware that resulted from the tragic death of the teen; it prohibits the use of *Salvia divinorum* in that state.) Because it is inexpensive and relatively easy to get, parents and lawmakers fear that its use could become more widespread.

As of April 2010, seventeen states had passed laws regulating salvia, and two others are considering, or have considered, a ban.

CHAPTER 2

THE EFFECTS OF MARIJUANA ON THE BODY

Your lungs convert the air you breathe into the oxygen and other gases your body needs to keep you alive. Those gases are transferred directly into your blood from your lungs. If you inhale smoke, the ingredients in that smoke are carried into your lungs and blood when you breathe. It's the same process whether you're breathing pure mountain air, city smog, or smoke from a house fire, cigarettes, or a joint. Your lungs also remove polluted air from your body. When you breathe out, you exhale carbon

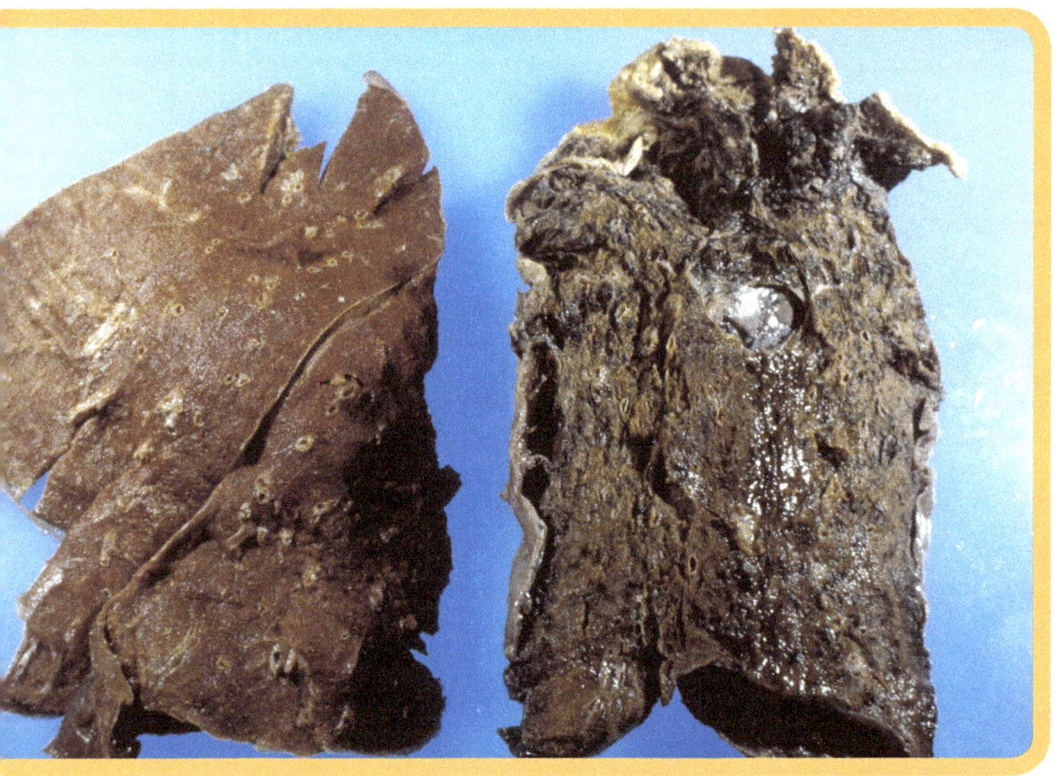

A person's normal lung *(left)* is shown beside a smoker's lung *(right)*. Smoking marijuana can cause major lung damage because smokers inhale deeply and long. Coughing, wheezing, and chronic bronchitis are just a few of its possible side effects.

dioxide, a waste product your body needs to get rid of. This transfer of clean air in and unclean air out is made possible by the tiny, delicate air sacs inside your lungs, called alveoli. Alveoli are found at the end of the bronchial tubes. These air sacs are very soft and vulnerable, and in order to work correctly, they have to stay clean, flexible, and healthy. Alveoli can become seriously infected when exposed to smoke, contributing to diseases like pneumonia and bronchitis. They are meant to filter gases, not the tiny, solid pieces of matter that come in with polluted air, smoke, or air filled with pollen.

To get an idea of what this means, look at the lint filter on a clothes dryer. Air moves through it to dry the clothes, but lint from the clothes is trapped by the screen. If you don't clean that filter, the dryer won't work right and the clothes won't get dry. It might even start a fire. Now, it would be great if smokers could just pull out their lungs and roll off the residue from smoking the way you can remove lint from a lint filter, but it doesn't work that way. At first, tiny hairlike cilia on the insides of the bronchial tubes work hard to push the solids back up so that the person can cough them out. But over time, smoking damages the cilia, so they can't do their job anymore. All that residue just builds up in there, keeping the smoker's lungs from working right.

Links to Physical Disorders

By now, everyone knows how unhealthy cigarette smoking is. People know that cigarettes put tar and nicotine into their body, coating their lungs with cancer-causing gunk and getting their brain addicted to smoking. Scientists have identified many cancer-causing ingredients in tobacco cigarettes, and many of those ingredients are also in marijuana. Some of those ingredients are stronger or more concentrated in pot than they are in cigarettes. Marijuana also contains THC, which is an irritant to the lungs. On top of all that, people who smoke it tend to inhale even more deeply than tobacco smokers do, and they actually hold their breath to keep the smoke in their lungs and get high faster. This allows all of those disease-causing ingredients to do even more damage in a shorter amount of time.

Here are some examples of lung diseases you might get if you smoke tobacco or marijuana or if you are exposed to secondhand smoke from someone smoking around you:

Smoking Marijuana and the Reproductive System

Many marijuana users are not aware that smoking pot affects the reproductive system. It can change the level of sex hormones, influence your sexual development (it can even delay puberty), and actually determine whether or not you can have a baby. The body may store THC in the tissues of the reproductive organs. Medical researchers believe that the accumulation of this psychoactive chemical affects the level of hormones in frequent marijuana users, both women and men. In women, THC affects the sex hormones estrogen and progesterone, causing irregular menstrual cycles. In men, it lowers the level of testosterone, which reduces their sperm count. Irregular periods and a low sperm count are common reasons for infertility. Generally, sperm start to swim very fast when they get close to a woman's egg. This is known as hyperactivation. When the sperm are exposed to THC, they begin the hyperactivation process immediately, and they usually tire themselves out before they can reach the egg. If the sperm don't reach the egg to fertilize it, pregnancy cannot occur. Consequently, if you plan to have children some day, it would be wise to steer clear of marijuana.

This picture shows the bronchioles of the lungs without constriction *(top)* and with constriction *(bottom)*. In an asthma attack, airways become inflamed and cause coughing, difficulty breathing, and chest pain. Smoke can trigger an attack in people who have asthma.

Respiratory Conditions

Asthma is a potentially life-threatening condition that makes breathing difficult or impossible. A person who has an asthma attack can't get enough air into his or her lungs and may faint. Several things happen during an asthma attack—the bronchial tubes swell, the muscles around them squeeze tight, and mucus is trapped, causing the gasping feeling that is so frightening to asthma sufferers and those watching them struggle to breathe. For people who have asthma, breathing any kind of smoke may trigger an attack.

As with asthma, emphysema makes you feel like you can't catch your breath. Your lungs become stiff, and the air sacs within them lose their ability to exchange the good air you breathe in with the carbon dioxide you breathe out. Your heart is forced to work much harder to compensate for the lack of oxygen coming in through your lungs. Eventually, your lungs or heart will just stop working and you will die trying to get enough air. Because emphysema develops slowly, you will most likely suffer years of pain, exhaustion, and being stuck with an oxygen tank and a wheelchair. Emphysema is incurable and is most often caused by smoking.

Lung Cancer

Lung cancer is almost always fatal. It usually spreads to other parts of the body before it is detected. Dying from lung cancer

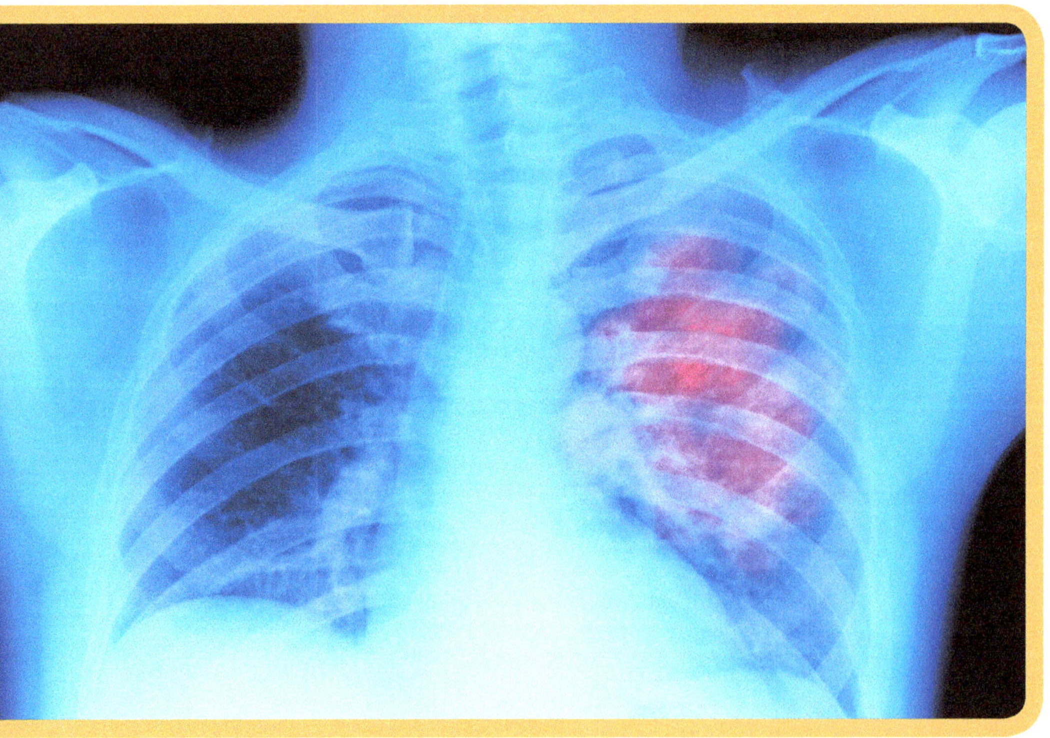

An X-ray of a person's chest indicates lung cancer. Despite the fact that marijuana contains many of the same toxins as tobacco, it has not been specifically tied to lung cancer.

is extremely painful, and it usually spreads. As someone with lung cancer becomes sicker, their lungs become weak and begin to fill with fluid. They begin to make an eerie sound as they breathe, called a death rattle. Since it's so hard to breathe, lung cancer victims cough a lot. Every time they cough, you would swear they are going to die from the effort. When they're not coughing, their breathing is very loud and strained and crackly sounding. If someone in your house has lung cancer, you will be able to hear their death-rattle breathing and their coughing throughout the entire house. In many cases, lung cancer victims actually die by drowning when fluids from inside their bodies seep into their lungs and fill them up. Lung cancer is the most common cause of death from cancer for both men and women. Although it is a subject of intense debate, the largest study of its kind recently found that despite sharing many of the same toxins, marijuana cannot be linked to lung cancer like tobacco is.

Accidents

Tobacco and marijuana have a lot of the same physical dangers, but marijuana use has an additional risk: accidents. Because smoking pot makes you clumsy and uncoordinated, makes you react more slowly, and makes you more likely to take risks, the chances of getting hurt in some sort of accident increase when you're high.

MYTHS & FACTS

MYTH Marijuana is not as bad for you as cigarettes.

FACT Marijuana actually contains many of the same cancer-causing chemicals that are found in tobacco. In fact, the levels of tar and carbon monoxide inhaled in pot smoke can be three to five times greater than what cigarette smokers breathe in. It is especially harmful because pot smokers tend to hold the smoke in their lungs for a long time.

MYTH Marijuana is not addictive.

FACT People used to think that marijuana was not addictive in the same way that other illegal drugs are. New research shows that this is not the case. People who use marijuana heavily can experience withdrawal symptoms when they stop using it for a period of time.

MYTH Marijuana will make you happy.

FACT You won't be very happy when your loved ones are disappointed in you or when you get suspended or expelled from school. How would you like to see your parents thrown in jail because you kept drugs in their house? All of these things could happen if you use marijuana. Some people find the high they get from smoking marijuana to be fun, but to those around them who are not high, they usually look pretty dumb. Not everyone enjoys being high. Some people get really scared from pot and have panic attacks. Some people become completely paranoid and convinced that everyone around them is out to get them.

CHAPTER 3

THE EFFECTS OF MARIJUANA ON THE BRAIN

Marijuana is a mind-altering drug. It changes the chemistry of the body and slows the thinking process. Because of that, many people think it helps them relax. They think it helps them stay calm. It doesn't.

In the body, THC makes the heart beat faster. It may beat from 80 beats a minute to 150. The air tubes in the lungs relax and become larger. More oxygen enters the blood. This extra oxygen is what causes the high.

Other blood vessels relax, too. The vessels in the eyes become larger and receive more blood. That makes the eyes red. When the vessels in the rest of the body relax, the blood pressure goes down. This drop makes the hands and feet feel cold. The low blood pressure also causes a light-headed feeling because not enough blood is reaching the brain.

The THC in the brain causes changes in the user's senses. Suddenly, the user may feel extremely thirsty or hungry. The

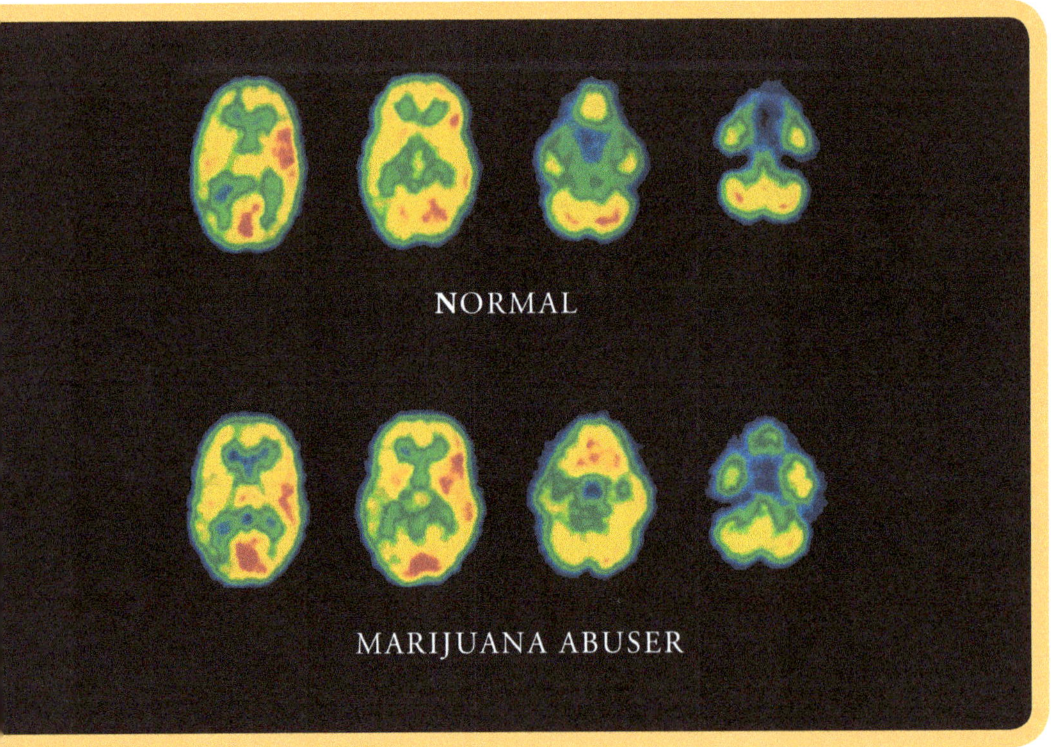

In a marijuana abuser's brain scans *(bottom)*, reduced brain activity can be seen when compared to a nonuser's brain scans *(top)*. The red area in the normal scans displays high brain activity, which is missing in the marijuana user's scans. The decreased activity in the bottom scans indicates a lack of coordination and poor spatial judgment.

"munchies" hit, and the user wants to eat everything in sight. The drug also distorts the way things appear. Many people think it makes them see art or hear music better. In fact, it only changes the appearance.

Even though medical researchers can show that these effects are bad, many people still want to use the drug. That is because for a short time it does make them feel good. When it is smoked, the user can feel light-headed and silly for about an hour. When it is eaten, the effect lasts for about four hours. Sometimes people want to feel that way. At parties and with friends, they laugh and have a good time when they are high on drugs. After the silliness is over, the drug makes the user feel sleepy. Some users feel that way from the start. People react differently to the drug. They may want more so that they can keep the high, or they may be depressed as they come down.

Often people who are stoned become exceedingly paranoid. They are certain that they are going to get arrested at any moment, that the police are watching them, or that their parents know what's going on. Sometimes the insecurities of the user come to light, and the user is convinced that everyone is saying bad things about him or her.

The morning after getting high, many people experience something similar to a hangover from alcohol, but without the nausea. This is often called being burnt. Burnt people experience all the disorientation and slowed thinking of being stoned, with none of the giggles. Sometimes this difficulty in clear thinking can last for a week or longer.

Marijuana and Driving

Using marijuana affects a person's ability to drive. According to a study conducted by the U.S. National Highway Traffic Safety Administration, a person's ability to drive safely is impaired by even just a small amount of marijuana. Participants in the study performed poorly when it came to reaction time and adjusting their speed to go along with the flow of traffic. In addition, they were less aware of their surroundings, including adjacent cars on the road. Drivers are much more dangerous to themselves and others when they lack safe driving skills. Not using good judgment puts a driver at greater risk for mishaps and physical injury.

Smoking even a tiny amount of marijuana can impair a person's ability to drive a car safely.

There are many reasons people would ignore all the nasty things about marijuana and smoke it. Here are some of the factors that make people turn to marijuana:

Lethargy

To a teenager, school sometimes seems meaningless. Some of the things that are taught don't seem to have much to do with real life. For that reason, many teenagers want to forget about school. They want to find something more exciting. Often drugs are their answer, but they don't have to be.

Many other things can be fun. Most schools have clubs or after-school activities. Many groups outside of school offer hobbies and sports. Religious orders often provide programs for teenagers. Most city and town governments offer projects for them. There is always something to interest you if you look hard enough.

Becoming involved in other things takes away the need for drugs. Drugs seem to offer escape from boredom and lethargy, but if you are doing lots of things, you won't have time to get bored. Have you thought about what you want to do when you finish high school? It's never too early to begin planning for the kind of life you want to lead.

Anxiety

Many people think that marijuana will help them relax if they are worried, feeling nervous, or uneasy about something. It

Find healthy ways to relieve stress instead of turning to marijuana. Doing yoga exercises might help you relax and feel less anxious.

does change the body and blood makeup so that it seems that the body is relaxing. In fact, it causes low blood pressure, and that causes more stress to the body. Because the senses are changed, the mind feels relaxed. There are safer ways to relax. The best part about them is that they do not cost any money. The library has many books about exercises that help you relax if you are feeling anxious or under a lot of stress. Some health insurance plans that parents have through their job offer stress release programs, such as biofeedback and meditation.

City parks and public groups offer other activities and classes that relieve stress. Yoga, tai chi, judo, and karate are examples. Many religious groups offer classes in meditation and learning how to relax. These are all healthy and safe ways to control stress.

Emotional Distress

Emotional or psychological pain is always hard to handle. When people begin to feel that life is nothing but hurt, they see drugs as an escape from that hurt. This is sometimes referred to as self-medicating. Drugs seem to be able to make all the distress go away. However, the pain always reappears. You can't stay high all the time. If you try, you will find yourself with more problems than when you began. You can never escape your problems. You have to deal with them or they will follow you forever.

Marijuana seems like the perfect drug for when life gets to be too much. It makes you happy, giggly, and so spaced out that you forget all your problems. Your problems are there even when you're high, and getting high just makes it impossible for you to deal with them. The paranoia that pot tends to cause can also make your problems seem even larger than they are. The mental confusion it causes in many people makes it impossible to cope. There are better ways to help yourself than through drugs. They give you another problem: your drug use. They make you weaker, both in mind and in body.

You never have to handle your problems on your own, especially if you find that they are taking over your life. You can talk to your parents, if they're not the source of the problem. You can talk to your teachers and counselors. You can call a hotline. There is help out there that will solve your problems, not just hide them for a night.

Fitting In

There is no rule that says you have to smoke dope to be a good friend or fit in with a group of friends. Sometimes people think that because others are doing something, they should, too. Everyone else may be doing it because they think it is the thing to do, not because they really want to.

Imagine your best friends. Would you try to talk them into jumping off a twenty-story building? Would you send them into

Don't bully someone because he or she does not fit into your group of friends. Likewise, if you are the one picked on for not smoking pot with your peers, perhaps you should reassess whether these people are your true friends.

someone's yard if there was a mean dog growling? No. You care about your friends and want them to be safe and happy. If that is true, what kind of a friend are you if you talk someone into taking drugs? What kind of people are your friends if they try to talk you into taking drugs?

Consider also that sometimes friends want you to try something they have done because if you do it, too, they will feel better about their actions. If they can get you to do it, maybe it's not so bad. If they say, "Well, everyone is smoking pot. It won't hurt me," you might try to trick yourself into believing it. That is why so many of your friends want you to try drugs with them. Not because they really think it's so hot. Not because they want to hurt you. They think if they can get everyone to do it, it won't seem like such a bad thing.

If you are trying to quit the habit, it is easier to stay clean if you hang around with people who do not use drugs. Perhaps you don't know anyone who does not use them. That will make trying to quit tough. There are places where you can go to meet other people. Schools have after-school activities where you can meet new friends. Large cities have community centers where teens can meet with other teens to talk. Religious groups have teen programs and offer many interesting activities.

Self-Respect

It takes more than marijuana to make you feel good about yourself. Drugs can give you a false sense of esteem. When you are high, you can pretend to be someone you're not. You usually end up looking more foolish than poised. You think you are acting normal. Most people who are sober can tell when someone has been taking marijuana. It has a potent odor for one thing. It also makes your eyes red and affects your behavior.

If you are nervous before an important event, there are other methods you can use to build pride and confidence. Meditation, deep breathing exercises, and positive thinking help. Affirmations are very powerful tools also. An affirmation is a positive statement you repeat to yourself over and over again until you believe it. For example, if you are nervous about an upcoming job interview, you could repeat to yourself: "I will be hired. I am confident. I will be hired. I am confident." Having the feeling that you are behaving with honor and dignity means that you also have self-respect.

Positive thinking helps build self-esteem. Instead of focusing on your faults, try to see all of the good things about yourself. To use our previous example, think of all the reasons you should get the job. Then when you are interviewed, those things will be in your mind and will show through.

Imagination

Some teens use drugs because they think it makes them more creative or imaginative. You hear people say all the time that getting high makes the music sound better. They also say they see colors and art with more vision. This is not actually true.

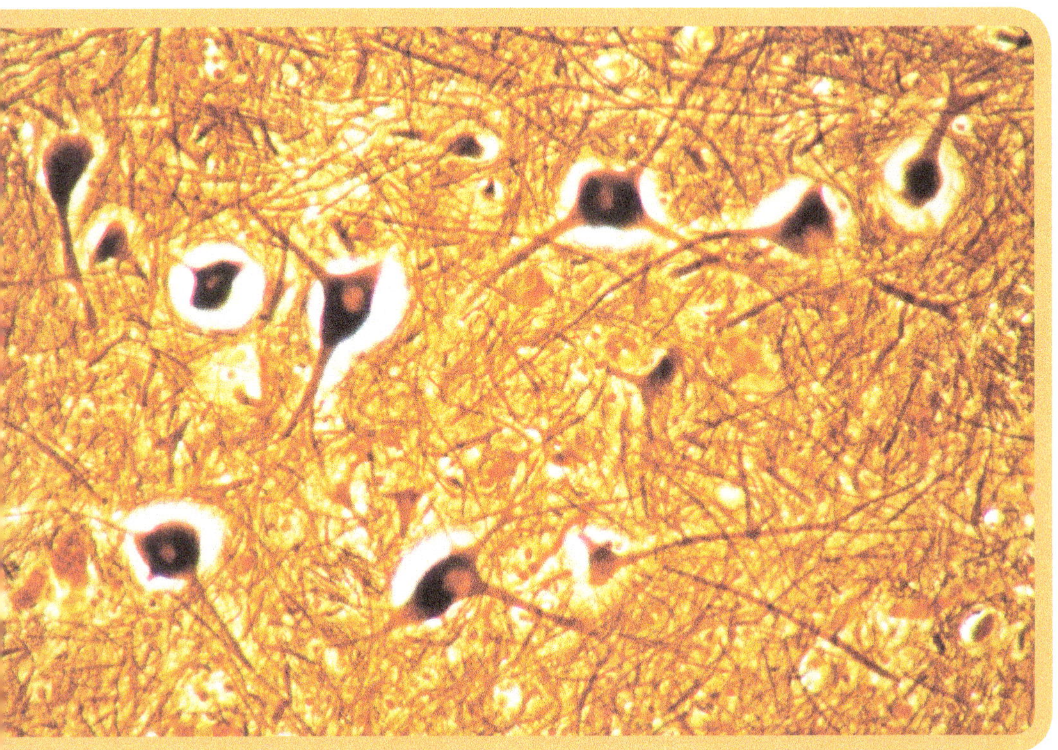

Smoking marijuana can destroy the brain's nerve cells, which are pictured here. Teens' developing brains are particularly vulnerable to the bad effects of pot. According to the *New York Times*, young adults who started using pot regularly in their early teens performed significantly worse on tests that studied brain function than did teens who were at least sixteen when they started.

The drug alters the mind so that it thinks music sounds better. It also changes vision so that colors seem brighter.

The truth is that while users think they are making their vision more clear, they are actually destroying the brain cells that are used to see. Memory loss is a proven side effect of marijuana use. If a user's goal is to be more creative and have a vivid imagination, he or she is actually being less creative and imaginative.

Marijuana also makes one groggy and sleepy when it starts wearing off. Sleepiness is certainly not creative, but is very typical of marijuana users.

Spiritual Insights

Another thing that attracts teenagers to marijuana is its use in the spiritual sense. Some teens and adults are searching for the meaning of life or who God is. Often they think that by altering their mind, they will gain the ability to have spiritual insights into these matters.

If this is an attraction to you, there are better ways to find answers to the reason for living. Every major religion has classes that offer answers. They also have people who are trained to help teens with these questions as well as those of everyday living.

CHAPTER 4

MARIJUANA'S OTHER ISSUES

If you smoke marijuana or do any other illegal drugs, you will have a hard time getting a job. It's not just the high-paying jobs that do drug testing now—some fast-food restaurants, car washes, and grocery stores do it, too. Employers don't want to hire people who are going to blow off work because they are stoned or come to work high and have accidents that will cost the company money.

Sports teams test for drugs, too. Athletes aren't allowed to use any drugs, such as steroids, that will make them perform

A human hair has been magnified by a scanning microscope. Authorities perform drug tests on a hair sample because marijuana and other drugs never come out of your hair once you are a drug user.

better than other players, and they're not allowed to use any illegal drugs like marijuana. If you want to be on any kind of team, you have to stay off drugs.

Before you start thinking you can smoke pot and get it out of your system before you have to take a drug test, think again. Drug testing is getting much more sophisticated and harder to beat. The THC in pot is absorbed mostly in fatty tissues and can be detected in urine tests a month or more after you use it.

Can Marijuana Be Addictive?

Marijuana dependence can be very similar to other substance dependence disorders, although many doctors and research scientists believe that the long-term effects of marijuana can be less severe. There is a major debate about whether someone can be addicted to marijuana. Some believe that a user can become addicted; others do not. Some users can stop at any time and not feel negative effects, while others cannot. Some believe that pot is only psychologically addictive, that people use it out of habit. When someone is dependent on a drug and then goes off it, they experience withdrawal, a physical and mental sickness. Medical studies have shown that long-time pot smokers who quit using marijuana experience withdrawal symptoms, including anxiousness and a bad temper. Some additional measures that doctors use in determining whether a drug is addictive are as follows:

Intoxication—the substance gets a user high

Reinforcement—the substance provides euphoria, a state of intense happiness and excitement, and it makes the user want to continue taking it

Tolerance—the more the user takes the drug, the more his or her body and mind get used to it, so the user has to take more of the substance to satisfy the need for it

Dependence—the user has a difficult time quitting or is unable to quit taking the drug, and the user has to depend on it to make him or her feel normal

Based on these criteria, doctors and researchers have determined that marijuana is mildly addictive, at the very least. The addiction can be stronger in some users than in others because of people's genetic differences.

So you might think you can just stay away from pot for the month before you know you'll be tested. However, many drug-testing companies are now using hair samples because drugs never come out of your hair. It's not just on your hair—it's actually in it. Because your hair grows only about half an inch (1.3 centimeters) per month, hair analysis can detect drugs you used more than a year ago.

You don't even have to smoke pot yourself for it to show up in your system. If you are around when other people are smoking it, you breathe in their secondhand smoke and your body absorbs it. There's even a new test that can detect microscopic amounts on your hands, so even if you don't actually use marijuana, you might still be penalized for hanging out with people who do.

Who Are Your Friends?

You might have noticed that the people who do drugs stick together and don't mix very much with the people who don't. You have to decide: Are you going to use drugs, or are you going to be drug-free? That decision will also decide for you who your friends will be. Do you want to hang out with people who are motivated and involved with life, or do you want to be with those who block out life's opportunities by getting high? Be careful—when you are with a group of people who think drugs are great, they will keep telling you how great drugs are and it will be really hard for you to resist joining in. You will never be able to convince them that drugs are bad. So, why are you with them?

Personal Hygiene

Another issue that can make people want to avoid you if you do smoke pot is your personal hygiene. When people

Marijuana abusers frequently become lethargic and fail to take care of their personal hygiene, physical appearance, and health. They often do not care how they behave or what happens to them.

use marijuana, their eyes get red and glassy, and their teeth become a brownish color. Besides smelling like pot smoke, which sticks to clothing and hair, users often neglect their physical appearance and health because they are so lethargic. Consequently, people you care about, your good friends and family members, might want to avoid being around you.

Dependence and Withdrawal

One of the worst behavioral issues that can result from being a marijuana user is becoming dependent on the substance. Addiction to a drug happens when a person feels normal only when he or she takes the drug routinely. The unnatural substances that are found in drugs can trick the brain into thinking it is getting normal amounts of natural chemicals. When a person takes drugs, the extra chemicals are added to those that the brain already makes. The brain then tries to adjust to the higher levels by decreasing the amount of chemicals that it ordinarily produces. Therefore, the level of natural chemicals becomes too low. The marijuana user has to use more to get the chemical levels up and the brain back on course.

CHAPTER 5

ADMITTING YOU HAVE A PROBLEM AND FINDING HELP

Although some people say that marijuana is harmless, it is dangerous and illegal. In spite of the fact that the controversy over medical use of marijuana continues, scientific experts claim there is no evidence of its legitimate medicinal benefits. The National Institute on Drug Abuse reported in 2010 that scientists have confirmed that the marijuana plant contains particular ingredients that have some therapeutic potential for helping control nausea and relieve pain, encourage appetite, and reduce eye pressure. According to Donna Shalala, the former Secretary of Health and Human Services under President Bill Clinton, "Available research has concluded that [smoking] marijuana is dangerous to your health." If you use marijuana and want to quit, you may need help. Marijuana is not physically addictive the way some other drugs such as heroin and cocaine are, but it can be habit-forming.

The first and most important step in recovering from a marijuana habit is to admit that you have a problem. Many drug users deny that they have a drug problem. This prevents them from seeking help.

The next step is to tell someone that you need help. This, too, may be difficult to admit. It may also be hard to decide whom to turn to for help. You may be nervous about admitting drug use because it is against the law.

Your Family

Perhaps you want to ask your parents for their help, but you're afraid because you think they won't understand or that they will just punish you. Most parents are loving people who care deeply for their children. They want to help their children when they are in trouble.

Think carefully about how you will tell your parents. It can be helpful to write down what you want to say and memorize it. Pick a time when your guardian or parents are relaxed and can focus on what you're telling them. Your parents' initial

Asking a parent for help in kicking your marijuana habit might be challenging. Make sure you think about how you are going to tell your parents about your drug problem. Remember, you've already taken a huge step by admitting that you have a problem.

reaction may be shock or anger. However, once they calm down, they will try to help you or find professional help.

If you don't think your parents will understand, try someone else you can trust. This may be an older sibling, an aunt or uncle,

or even the parent of a close friend who has always been there for you.

A Member of the Clergy

Your priest, rabbi, or minister may not seem like an obvious choice, but he or she is there to help. Religious leaders have dedicated their lives to helping people. Believe it or not, you are probably not the first person who has turned to your religious leader for help with a drug problem. Don't be afraid to go to a religious leader because you think he or she will judge you. He or she will try to help you or will recommend a trained drug counselor for you to talk to. If you're not comfortable talking to your own religious leader, you can always go to another church or temple and speak to a person there.

Many temples and churches have programs geared to help teens with drug problems. Many of the people in these programs have received some kind of professional counseling. The best thing about being a part of a group like this is that they will accept you and try to help you no matter what your problems are.

Teens at a drug rehabilitation meeting talk to a counselor and one another about their experiences and learn methods for recovery. Often it helps to get encouragement from people who understand what you are feeling.

School Teacher or Guidance Counselor

Other people you can talk to are teachers or school guidance counselors. The teacher should be someone you like and can

talk to easily. More important, he or she should be someone you trust. Your teacher will support you and be able to refer you to a person or place where you can get help.

A guidance counselor is also a good person to turn to for help. He or she has plenty of experience helping students deal with many different problems.

Other Helpful Support

Sometimes it is helpful just to have an understanding friend to listen to you. Telling someone the truth can be a relief. Having the support of a good friend can be invaluable.

Your local telephone book is a great resource for finding help. You can find drug abuse hotlines listed under community service numbers. If you are not ready to tell someone face to face about your drug problem, call a hotline. You can talk to a trained counselor who will listen and offer you support. You don't have to give your name, and the counselor will not force you to do anything you're not ready for. They can offer advice on what you should do next and can also send you valuable information about drug abuse and how to recover from it. They may be able to recommend a local counselor or therapist whom you can talk to. Hotline counselors will even help you prepare yourself to tell your parents about your problem.

There are many people in your life that you can turn to for help. If you really want to successfully quit using marijuana, you need help. Don't be afraid to ask for it. Recovering from a marijuana habit is difficult, but not impossible, especially with the support of those around you.

TEN GREAT QUESTIONS TO ASK A DOCTOR

1. What should I do if I'm having trouble staying away from marijuana?

2. What kind of withdrawal symptoms should I expect after I stop using marijuana?

3. How can I get tested for damage to my brain and my body?

4. Is there anything I can do to reverse the damage from smoking marijuana?

5. How can I help my friends who are still getting high?

6. Do you know anyone I can talk to who has been through this before?

7. Can you recommend any activities to help me keep my mind off of smoking marijuana?

8. If my grades have suffered because of my marijuana abuse, is there someone who can help me get back on track at school?

9. Is there a program or a clinic that can help me stop using marijuana?

10. Can you recommend a therapist who can help me with my recovery?

GLOSSARY

addiction The compulsive feeling of need for a drug.

affirmation A positive statement made repeatedly until it is believed.

asthma A condition in which the bronchial tubes swell or close up, making breathing difficult or impossible.

biofeedback A method of mentally controlling the automatic body functions, such as heartbeat.

bummer A slang term for an unpleasant reaction to a drug that is expected to provide a high.

carcinogens Cancer-causing substances, such as those found in cigarettes and marijuana.

chemistry The chemical makeup and properties of the body and its various organs.

depressant A sedative or something that calms.

depression A deep feeling of sadness; can be temporary or of long duration.

glaucoma A condition of increased pressure in the eyeball that can cause gradual loss of vision.

infertility Not being able to reproduce.

infraction A violation of a law or set of rules.

lethargy A lack of energy and enthusiasm.

meditation The act of focusing the mind in order to change one's thoughts.

misdemeanor A minor wrongdoing; an offense that is less serious than a felony.

narcotic A drug that eases pain and alters the mind.

psychoactive Affecting the mind.

psychological pain Mental disturbance resulting from influences outside oneself.

roach The last tiny butt of a joint or reefer.

roach clip A clip or pin used to hold a roach.

spiritual Relating to things that are religious or supernatural.

stoned Being high on pot.

tetrahydrocannabinol (THC) The main chemical in marijuana that acts on the brain and causes the high and that is detected in drug tests.

vision Something seen in a dream or a trance.

yoga A system of physical activity designed to gain control of body or mind.

FOR MORE INFORMATION

Center for Substance Abuse Treatment
5600 Fishers Lane Rockwall II
Rockville, MD 20857
(301) 443-0365
Information and Treatment Referral Hotline:
(800) 729-6686
Web site: http://prevention.samhsa.gov
The center, which is part of the U.S. Department of Health and Human Services, promotes the quality and availability of community-based substance abuse treatment services for individuals and families who need them.

Drug and Alcohol Treatment Infoline
(800) 565-8603
Web site: http://www.dart.on.ca
This drug information line is staffed twenty-four hours a day, seven days a week.

Hazelden
15251 Pleasant Valley Road
Center City, MN 55012
(866) 545-6439 or (800) 257-7810

Web site: http://www.hazelden.org
This nonprofit organization is dedicated to helping people recover from alcoholism and drug addiction.

Health Canada, Ontario Region
180 Queen Street West
Toronto, ON M5V 3L7
Canada
(866) 337-7705
Web site: http://www.hc-sc.gc.ca
Health Canada grants access to marijuana for medical use to those who are suffering from grave and debilitating illnesses. This Web site details the law enforcement issues and policies.

National Clearinghouse for Alcohol and Drug Information
11426–28 Rockville Pike, Suite 200
Rockville, MD 20852
(800) 729-6686
Web site: http://www.ncadi.samhsa.gov
This is a clearinghouse of reports and articles on drug abuse prevention and related information.

National Council on Alcoholism and Drug Dependence
12 West 21st Street, 7 Floor
New York, NY 10010

(800) 622-2255
Web site: http://www.ncadd.org
This organization promotes prevention, treatment, and recovery from alcoholism and drug addiction.

National Drug and Alcohol Treatment Referral Service
(800) 662-HELP (662-4357)
This service can link callers to a variety of hotlines that provide treatment referrals.

National Families in Action
Century Plaza II
2957 Clairmont Road, Suite 150
Atlanta, GA 30329
(404) 934-6364
Web site: http://www.emory.edu/NFIA
This organization's mission is to help families and communities prevent drug use among children by promoting policies based on science.

National Institute on Drug Abuse
5600 Fishers Lane, Room 10-05
Rockville, MD 20857
(301) 443-6480
Web site: http://www.nida.nih.gov
This agency supports and conducts research on drug abuse and addiction.

National Institute on Mental Health
5600 Fishers Lane, Room 17-99
Rockville, MD 20857
(301) 443-3673
Web site: http://www.nimh.nih.gov
This division of the National Institutes of Health conducts research nationally on mental illness and mental health, including studies of the brain, behavior, and mental health services.

Web Sites

Due to the changing nature of Internet links, Rosen Publishing has developed an online list of Web sites related to the subject of this book. This site is updated regularly. Please use this link to access the list:

http://www.rosenlinks.com/dac/mar

FOR FURTHER READING

Carroll, Jamuna, ed. *Opposing Viewpoints: Marijuana.* Chicago, IL: Greenhaven Press, 2005.

Gillard, Arthur. *Marijuana* (At Issue). Chicago, IL: Greenhaven Press, 2009.

Haley, John. *The Truth About Drugs*. 2nd ed. New York, NY: Facts On File, 2009.

Kane, Brigid M. *Marijuana* (Understanding Drugs). New York, NY: Chelsea House, 2011.

Marcovitz, Hal. *Marijuana* (Drug Education Library). Chicago, IL: Lucent Books, 2006.

Minamide, Elaine. *Medical Marijuana* (Issues That Concern You). Chicago, IL: Greenhaven Press, 2009.

Nagle, Jeanne. *Marijuana* (Incredibly Disgusting Drugs). New York, NY: Rosen Publishing, 2008.

Nakaya, Andrea C. *Marijuana*. San Diego, CA: ReferencePoint Press, 2007.

Pearson, Felicia. *Grace After Midnight: A Memoir.* New York, NY: Grand Central Publishing, 2007.

Sheff, David. *Beautiful: A Father's Journey Through His Son's Addiction*. Boston, MA: Houghton Mifflin, 2008.

Sonnenberg, Susanna. *Her Last Death: A Memoir.* New York, NY: Scribner, 2008.

Van Tuyl, Christine. *Marijuana*. Detroit, MI: Cengage Gale, 2007.

INDEX

About the Authors

Frederick C. Gross is a writer who resides in Grand Rapids, Michigan.

Reeve Chace earned an undergraduate degree in English literature and sociology from Middlebury College in Vermont and a graduate degree in public health, with a concentration in community health education, from Hunter College in New York City. She has worked in medical research at Mount Sinai School of Medicine and lives in New York City.

Photo Credits

Cover, p. 1 © boojus/www.istockphoto.com; pp. 4–5 istockphoto/Thinkstock; pp. 8, 14, 21, 29, 42, 48, 56, 58, 62, 63 DEA; pp. 10–11 Hemera/Thinkstock; pp. 14–15 Jupiterimages/Workbook Stock/Getty Images; p. 16 © AP Images; p. 19 Brian Baer/MCT/Landov; p. 22 Arthur Glauberman/Photo Researchers; p. 25 AJPhoto/Photo Researchers; p. 26 Peter Dazeley/The Image Bank/Getty Images; p. 30 Pascal Goetgheluck/SPL/Custom Medical Stock Photo; pp. 32, 34 Shutterstock; pp. 36–37 SW Productions/Photodisc/Getty Images; p. 40 Image Source/Getty Images; p. 43 Steve Gschmeissner/Photo Researchers; p. 46 © Daniel Rodriguez/www.istockphoto.com; pp. 50–51 Jupiterimages/Pixland/Thinkstock; pp. 52–53 © Mary Kate Denny/Photo Edit.

Photo Researcher: Marty Levick